OUR FAMILY HISTORY

This Book Belongs To:

OUR FAMILY HISTORY

AVENEL BOOKS · NEW YORK

Published by Avenel Books, distributed by
Crown Publishers, Inc.
One Park Avenue
New York, New York 10016

h g f e d c b

❧CONTENTS❧

※ INTRODUCTION ※

In these modern times when it appears that you are losing touch with the value of strong family ties and the solid foundation of your identity, tracing your ancestry can become an important link with the past.

Genealogy became fashionable long before the advent of the written word, when stories were handed down from generation to generation. The Egyptians etched the legacy of pharaohs and religious men in stone. The Greeks and Romans zealously researched their heritage to support claims to higher levels of society. In the Middle Ages, nobility, affluence, and real estate all hinged on proof of heritage. Heraldry, using coats of arms on shields, banners, and garments flourished during this time.

What once was restricted to aristocratic families, who employed historians to trace their distinguished lineage, is now available to anyone interested in investigating his family origins. "Finding your roots" has taken on wider proportions and has become an honorable avocation for all types of people on all social levels throughout the world.

Indeed, charting your family tree weaves the past and present, revealing new facets of your history. It establishes a bond with people you never met and with events that are locked in another time, beyond reach and understanding. Every family pedigree will unravel a unique history, a personal generational drama. You will discover that every twist and turn of your family tree has some bearing on your appearance and your behavior and can become a vital force in the future.

Imagine your surprise as you discover the unexpected characters, the scandal, the intrigue, the unheralded achievements, the stories that are not found in history books but are unequivocally more significant to your own personal history. Time can fade and distort events, grand and small. With complete and accurate family records, events can be recalled in vibrant detail.

In searching out the missing links in your family chain, perseverence is needed to get you through the times when your research results in a dead end. But the discovery of a new branch on your family tree or an interesting forebear is a great reward for your patience. The importance of establishing complete and precise family records is apparent. You are the sum of your ancestors' traits and characteristics, and those who follow you will regard you as their link to history. Just as you have been your own detective, tracking down clues in attics, cellars, closets, and libraries, through newspapers, yellowed letters, and brown-edged pictures, your records will provide the answers to crucial genealogical questions that may surface in some future search for family connections.

Our Family History is designed to assist you in a successful genealogical search as well as provide a volume in which to record your own personal account of your family's lives. The first section, "Ancestry & Family Trees," includes a basic chart for you to reconstruct your family tree. The clear, concise format will reveal the lines of descent previously hidden amongst its tangled and interwoven roots. Also included are pages for listing your descendants, progenitors, and relations.

"Family History" is an extensive section that includes specific pages for information about family gatherings, vacations, and traditions in addition to the other treasured accounts in your family's life. Family gatherings are the ceremonies of generational bonds. *Our Family History* lets you record the anniversaries, graduations, homecomings, and other joyous events shared by loved ones. Logging your family vacations is a way of remembering the places and the people that made that special time so memorable. In every family, unique traditions are the legacy passed from one generation to the next. This heritage might take the form of favorite family recipes, time-honored bedtime stories, or a particular way of celebrating holidays. Entering your family's traditions on these pages will preserve these special rites and rituals for decades to come.

"Family Records & Documents" is a section to aid you in recording the specific locations of wills, insurance policies, treasured portraits, valuable paintings, family heirlooms, stock certificates, and deeds to family property. Pages are included as well for family medical histories and cemetery records.

Use "Family Interviews" as the place to preserve the thoughts, feelings, and recollections that bind families together. This section is a precious reminder for generations to come of the memories of times past, often the most perishable of inheritances. The interviews help make this volume a storehouse of family lore.

Our Family History is designed so that anyone can become his family's historian. Its flexibility makes it a perfect gift for the new baby, newlyweds, or proud grandparents. It is not only a gift of life, but a gift of love.

George Gesner

ANCESTRY & FAMILY TREES

IMMEDIATE FAMILY

Father

full name
_____

date of birth
_____

place of birth
_____

Mother

full name
_____

date of birth
_____

place of birth
_____

Married

date
_____

place
_____

by
_____

witnesses or attendants
_____

Children

full name
_____

date of birth
_____

place of birth
_____

full name
_____

date of birth
_____

place of birth
_____

full name
_____

date of birth
_____

place of birth
_____

full name
_____

date of birth
_____

place of birth
_____

full name
_____

date of birth
_____

place of birth
_____

full name
_____

date of birth
_____

place of birth
_____

full name
_____

date of birth
_____

place of birth
_____

full name
_____

date of birth
_____

place of birth
_____

HUSBAND'S ANCESTRAL CHART

FATHER'S ANCESTRY

father's full name

date of birth   place of birth

date of marriage   place of marriage

date of death   place of burial

occupation

husband's full name

date of birth   place of birth

date of death   place of burial

occupation

husband's brothers and sisters

MOTHER'S ANCESTRY

mother's full name

date of birth   place of birth

date of marriage   place of marriage

date of death   place of burial

occupation

grandfather's full name

date of birth   place of birth

date of marriage   place of marriage

date of death   place of burial

occupation

grandmother's full name

date of birth   place of birth

date of marriage   place of marriage

date of death   place of burial

occupation

grandfather's full name

date of birth   place of birth

date of marriage   place of marriage

date of death   place of burial

occupation

grandmother's full name

date of birth   place of birth

date of marriage   place of marriage

date of death   place of burial

occupation

great grandfather's full name
_____
date of birth   place of birth
_____
occupation
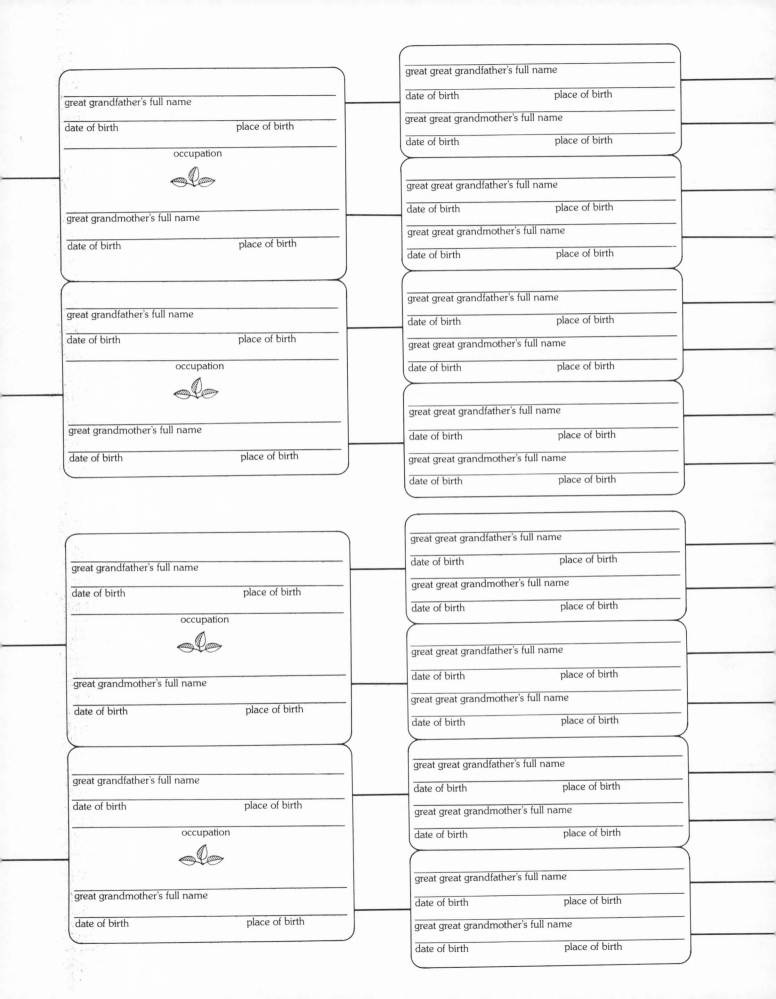

great grandmother's full name
_____
date of birth   place of birth

great great grandfather's full name
_____
date of birth   place of birth
_____
great great grandmother's full name
_____
date of birth   place of birth

great great grandfather's full name
_____
date of birth   place of birth
_____
great great grandmother's full name
_____
date of birth   place of birth

great grandfather's full name
_____
date of birth   place of birth
_____
occupation

great grandmother's full name
_____
date of birth   place of birth

great great grandfather's full name
_____
date of birth   place of birth
_____
great great grandmother's full name
_____
date of birth   place of birth

great great grandfather's full name
_____
date of birth   place of birth
_____
great great grandmother's full name
_____
date of birth   place of birth

great grandfather's full name
_____
date of birth   place of birth
_____
occupation

great grandmother's full name
_____
date of birth   place of birth

great great grandfather's full name
_____
date of birth   place of birth
_____
great great grandmother's full name
_____
date of birth   place of birth

great great grandfather's full name
_____
date of birth   place of birth
_____
great great grandmother's full name
_____
date of birth   place of birth

great grandfather's full name
_____
date of birth   place of birth
_____
occupation

great grandmother's full name
_____
date of birth   place of birth

great great grandfather's full name
_____
date of birth   place of birth
_____
great great grandmother's full name
_____
date of birth   place of birth

great great grandfather's full name
_____
date of birth   place of birth
_____
great great grandmother's full name
_____
date of birth   place of birth

great great great grandfather's full name — date of marriage
great great great grandmother's full name — nee*
great great great grandfather's full name — date of marriage
great great great grandmother's full name — nee

great great great grandfather's full name — date of marriage
great great great grandmother's full name — nee
great great great grandfather's full name — date of marriage
great great great grandmother's full name — nee

great great great grandfather's full name — date of marriage
great great great grandmother's full name — nee
great great great grandfather's full name — date of marriage
great great great grandmother's full name — nee

great great great grandfather's full name — date of marriage
great great great grandmother's full name — nee
great great great grandfather's full name — date of marriage
great great great grandmother's full name — nee

great great great grandfather's full name — date of marriage
great great great grandmother's full name — nee
great great great grandfather's full name — date of marriage
great great great grandmother's full name — nee

great great great grandfather's full name — date of marriage
great great great grandmother's full name — nee
great great great grandfather's full name — date of marriage
great great great grandmother's full name — nee

great great great grandfather's full name — date of marriage
great great great grandmother's full name — nee
great great great grandfather's full name — date of marriage
great great great grandmother's full name — nee

great great great grandfather's full name — date of marriage
great great great grandmother's full name — nee
great great great grandfather's full name — date of marriage
great great great grandmother's full name — nee

*nee represents wife's maiden name

WIFE'S ANCESTRAL CHART

FATHER'S ANCESTRY

father's full name

date of birth   place of birth

date of marriage   place of marriage

date of death   place of burial

occupation

grandfather's full name

date of birth   place of birth

date of marriage   place of marriage

date of death   place of burial

occupation

grandmother's full name

date of birth   place of birth

date of marriage   place of marriage

date of death   place of burial

occupation

wife's full name

date of birth   place of birth

date of death   place of burial

occupation

wife's brothers and sisters

MOTHER'S ANCESTRY

mother's full name

date of birth   place of birth

date of marriage   place of marriage

date of death   place of burial

occupation

grandfather's full name

date of birth   place of birth

date of marriage   place of marriage

date of death   place of burial

occupation

grandmother's full name

date of birth   place of birth

date of marriage   place of marriage

date of death   place of burial

occupation

great grandfather's full name

date of birth   place of birth

occupation

great grandmother's full name

date of birth   place of birth

---

great grandfather's full name

date of birth   place of birth

occupation

great grandmother's full name

date of birth   place of birth

---

great grandfather's full name

date of birth   place of birth

occupation

great grandmother's full name

date of birth   place of birth

---

great grandfather's full name

date of birth   place of birth

occupation

great grandmother's full name

date of birth   place of birth

---

great great grandfather's full name

date of birth   place of birth

great great grandmother's full name

date of birth   place of birth

---

great great grandfather's full name

date of birth   place of birth

great great grandmother's full name

date of birth   place of birth

---

great great grandfather's full name

date of birth   place of birth

great great grandmother's full name

date of birth   place of birth

---

great great grandfather's full name

date of birth   place of birth

great great grandmother's full name

date of birth   place of birth

---

great great grandfather's full name

date of birth   place of birth

great great grandmother's full name

date of birth   place of birth

---

great great grandfather's full name

date of birth   place of birth

great great grandmother's full name

date of birth   place of birth

---

great great grandfather's full name

date of birth   place of birth

great great grandmother's full name

date of birth   place of birth

---

great great grandfather's full name

date of birth   place of birth

great great grandmother's full name

date of birth   place of birth

great great great grandfather's full name	date of marriage
great great great grandmother's full name	nee*
great great great grandfather's full name	date of marriage
great great great grandmother's full name	nee

great great great grandfather's full name	date of marriage
great great great grandmother's full name	nee
great great great grandfather's full name	date of marriage
great great great grandmother's full name	nee

great great great grandfather's full name	date of marriage
great great great grandmother's full name	nee
great great great grandfather's full name	date of marriage
great great great grandmother's full name	nee

great great great grandfather's full name	date of marriage
great great great grandmother's full name	nee
great great great grandfather's full name	date of marriage
great great great grandmother's full name	nee

great great great grandfather's full name	date of marriage
great great great grandmother's full name	nee
great great great grandfather's full name	date of marriage
great great great grandmother's full name	nee

great great great grandfather's full name	date of marriage
great great great grandmother's full name	nee
great great great grandfather's full name	date of marriage
great great great grandmother's full name	nee

great great great grandfather's full name	date of marriage
great great great grandmother's full name	nee
great great great grandfather's full name	date of marriage
great great great grandmother's full name	nee

great great great grandfather's full name	date of marriage
great great great grandmother's full name	nee
great great great grandfather's full name	date of marriage
great great great grandmother's full name	nee

*nee represents wife's maiden name

FAMILY RECORDER

full name _____

date of birth _____ place of birth _____ date of death _____ place of burial _____

father's full name _____ mother's full name _____

married to _____

Children
- name _____ born _____ died _____
- name _____ born _____ died _____
- name _____ born _____ died _____
- name _____ born _____ died _____
- name _____ born _____ died _____

Brothers & Sisters
- name _____ born _____ died _____
- name _____ born _____ died _____
- name _____ born _____ died _____
- name _____ born _____ died _____
- name _____ born _____ died _____

full name _____

date of birth _____ place of birth _____ date of death _____ place of burial _____

father's full name _____ mother's full name _____

married to _____

Children
- name _____ born _____ died _____
- name _____ born _____ died _____
- name _____ born _____ died _____
- name _____ born _____ died _____
- name _____ born _____ died _____

Brothers & Sisters
- name _____ born _____ died _____
- name _____ born _____ died _____
- name _____ born _____ died _____
- name _____ born _____ died _____
- name _____ born _____ died _____

full name

| date of birth | place of birth | date of death | place of burial |

father's full name   mother's full name

married to

Children

name		born	died
name		born	died
name		born	died
name		born	died
name		born	died

Brothers & Sisters

name		born	died
name		born	died
name		born	died
name		born	died
name		born	died

full name

| date of birth | place of birth | date of death | place of burial |

father's full name   mother's full name

married to

Children

name		born	died
name		born	died
name		born	died
name		born	died
name		born	died

Brothers & Sisters

name		born	died
name		born	died
name		born	died
name		born	died
name		born	died

full name
_____

date of birth _____ place of birth _____ date of death _____ place of burial _____

father's full name _____ mother's full name _____

married to _____

Children
name		born	died
name		born	died
name		born	died
name		born	died
name		born	died

Brothers & Sisters
name		born	died
name		born	died
name		born	died
name		born	died
name		born	died

full name
_____

date of birth _____ place of birth _____ date of death _____ place of burial _____

father's full name _____ mother's full name _____

married to _____

Children
name		born	died
name		born	died
name		born	died
name		born	died
name		born	died

Brothers & Sisters
name		born	died
name		born	died
name		born	died
name		born	died
name		born	died

full name
_____

date of birth _____ place of birth _____ date of death _____ place of burial _____

father's full name _____ mother's full name _____

married to _____

Children
name	born	died
name	born	died
name	born	died
name	born	died
name	born	died

Brothers & Sisters
name	born	died
name	born	died
name	born	died
name	born	died
name	born	died

full name
_____

date of birth _____ place of birth _____ date of death _____ place of burial _____

father's full name _____ mother's full name _____

married to _____

Children
name	born	died
name	born	died
name	born	died
name	born	died
name	born	died

Brothers & Sisters
name	born	died
name	born	died
name	born	died
name	born	died
name	born	died

full name

| date of birth | place of birth | date of death | place of burial |

father's full name | mother's full name

married to

Children

name	born	died
name	born	died
name	born	died
name	born	died
name	born	died

Brothers & Sisters

name	born	died
name	born	died
name	born	died
name	born	died
name	born	died

full name

| date of birth | place of birth | date of death | place of burial |

father's full name | mother's full name

married to

Children

name	born	died
name	born	died
name	born	died
name	born	died
name	born	died

Brothers & Sisters

name	born	died
name	born	died
name	born	died
name	born	died
name	born	died

full name

date of birth	place of birth	date of death	place of burial

father's full name   mother's full name

married to

Children

name	born	died
name	born	died
name	born	died
name	born	died
name	born	died

Brothers
& Sisters

name	born	died
name	born	died
name	born	died
name	born	died
name	born	died

full name

date of birth	place of birth	date of death	place of burial

father's full name   mother's full name

married to

Children

name	born	died
name	born	died
name	born	died
name	born	died
name	born	died

Brothers
& Sisters

name	born	died
name	born	died
name	born	died
name	born	died
name	born	died

full name
_____

date of birth	place of birth	date of death	place of burial

father's full name   mother's full name
_____

married to
_____

Children

name	born	died
name	born	died
name	born	died
name	born	died
name	born	died

Brothers & Sisters

name	born	died
name	born	died
name	born	died
name	born	died
name	born	died

full name
_____

date of birth	place of birth	date of death	place of burial

father's full name   mother's full name
_____

married to
_____

Children

name	born	died
name	born	died
name	born	died
name	born	died
name	born	died

Brothers & Sisters

name	born	died
name	born	died
name	born	died
name	born	died
name	born	died

full name

| date of birth | place of birth | date of death | place of burial |

father's full name   mother's full name

married to

Children

name	born	died
name	born	died
name	born	died
name	born	died
name	born	died

Brothers
& Sisters

name	born	died
name	born	died
name	born	died
name	born	died
name	born	died

full name

| date of birth | place of birth | date of death | place of burial |

father's full name   mother's full name

married to

Children

name	born	died
name	born	died
name	born	died
name	born	died
name	born	died

Brothers
& Sisters

name	born	died
name	born	died
name	born	died
name	born	died
name	born	died

full name

date of birth	place of birth	date of death	place of burial

father's full name   mother's full name

married to

Children	name	born	died
	name	born	died
	name	born	died
	name	born	died
	name	born	died
Brothers & Sisters	name	born	died
	name	born	died
	name	born	died
	name	born	died
	name	born	died

full name

date of birth	place of birth	date of death	place of burial

father's full name   mother's full name

married to

Children	name	born	died
	name	born	died
	name	born	died
	name	born	died
	name	born	died
Brothers & Sisters	name	born	died
	name	born	died
	name	born	died
	name	born	died
	name	born	died

full name

| date of birth | place of birth | date of death | place of burial |

father's full name   mother's full name

married to

Children

name	born	died
name	born	died
name	born	died
name	born	died
name	born	died

Brothers & Sisters

name	born	died
name	born	died
name	born	died
name	born	died
name	born	died

full name

| date of birth | place of birth | date of death | place of burial |

father's full name   mother's full name

married to

Children

name	born	died
name	born	died
name	born	died
name	born	died
name	born	died

Brothers & Sisters

name	born	died
name	born	died
name	born	died
name	born	died
name	born	died

full name

date of birth	place of birth	date of death	place of burial

father's full name   mother's full name

married to

Children

name		born	died
name		born	died
name		born	died
name		born	died
name		born	died

Brothers & Sisters

name		born	died
name		born	died
name		born	died
name		born	died
name		born	died

full name

date of birth	place of birth	date of death	place of burial

father's full name   mother's full name

married to

Children

name		born	died
name		born	died
name		born	died
name		born	died
name		born	died

Brothers & Sisters

name		born	died
name		born	died
name		born	died
name		born	died
name		born	died

full name
_____

date of birth _____ place of birth _____ date of death _____ place of burial _____

father's full name _____ mother's full name _____

married to _____

Children

name	born	died
name	born	died
name	born	died
name	born	died
name	born	died

Brothers & Sisters

name	born	died
name	born	died
name	born	died
name	born	died
name	born	died

full name
_____

date of birth _____ place of birth _____ date of death _____ place of burial _____

father's full name _____ mother's full name _____

married to _____

Children

name	born	died
name	born	died
name	born	died
name	born	died
name	born	died

Brothers & Sisters

name	born	died
name	born	died
name	born	died
name	born	died
name	born	died

full name _____

date of birth	place of birth	date of death	place of burial

father's full name _____ mother's full name _____

married to _____

Children	name	born	died
	name	born	died
	name	born	died
	name	born	died
	name	born	died
Brothers & Sisters	name	born	died
	name	born	died
	name	born	died
	name	born	died
	name	born	died

full name _____

date of birth	place of birth	date of death	place of burial

father's full name _____ mother's full name _____

married to _____

Children	name	born	died
	name	born	died
	name	born	died
	name	born	died
	name	born	died
Brothers & Sisters	name	born	died
	name	born	died
	name	born	died
	name	born	died
	name	born	died

FAMILY
HISTORY

_____ and _____
husband   wife

_____   _____
date   place

_____   _____
ceremony conducted by   time of day

_____
religious/civil ceremony

_____
attendants

_____

_____

_____
guests

_____

_____

_____ and _____
husband   wife

_____   _____
date   place

_____   _____
ceremony conducted by   time of day

_____
religious/civil ceremony

_____
attendants

_____

_____

_____
guests

_____

_____

_____ and _____
husband   wife

_____
date   place

_____
ceremony conducted by   time of day

_____
religious/civil ceremony

_____
attendants

_____

_____

guests

_____

_____

_____ and _____
husband   wife

_____
date   place

_____
ceremony conducted by   time of day

_____
religious/civil ceremony

_____
attendants

_____

_____

guests

_____

_____

_____ and _____
husband   wife

_____
date   place

_____
ceremony conducted by   time of day

_____
religious/civil ceremony

_____
attendants

_____

_____

guests

_____

_____

_____ and _____
husband   wife

_____   _____
date   place

_____   _____
ceremony conducted by   time of day

_____
religious/civil ceremony

_____
attendants

_____

_____

_____
guests

_____

_____

_____ and _____
husband   wife

_____   _____
date   place

_____   _____
ceremony conducted by   time of day

_____
religious/civil ceremony

_____
attendants

_____

_____

_____
guests

_____

_____

_____ and _____
husband   wife

_____   _____
date   place

_____   _____
ceremony conducted by   time of day

_____
religious/civil ceremony

_____
attendants

_____

_____

_____
guests

_____

_____

OTHER RELIGIOUS CEREMONIES

description
_____

date   place
_____

ceremony conducted by
_____

description
_____

date   place
_____

ceremony conducted by
_____

description
_____

date   place
_____

ceremony conducted by
_____

description
_____

date   place
_____

ceremony conducted by
_____

description
_____

date   place
_____

ceremony conducted by
_____

description
_____

date   place
_____

ceremony conducted by
_____

description
_____

date _____ place _____

ceremony conducted by _____

description
_____

date _____ place _____

ceremony conducted by _____

description
_____

date _____ place _____

ceremony conducted by _____

description
_____

date _____ place _____

ceremony conducted by _____

description
_____

date _____ place _____

ceremony conducted by _____

description
_____

date _____ place _____

ceremony conducted by _____

description
_____

date _____ place _____

ceremony conducted by _____

description
_____

date   place
_____

ceremony conducted by
_____

description
_____

date   place
_____

ceremony conducted by
_____

description
_____

date   place
_____

ceremony conducted by
_____

description
_____

date   place
_____

ceremony conducted by
_____

description
_____

date   place
_____

ceremony conducted by
_____

description
_____

date   place
_____

ceremony conducted by
_____

description
_____

date   place
_____

ceremony conducted by
_____

FAMILY BIRTHS

name

mother   father

date   place

weight   height   attending physician

name

mother   father

date   place

weight   height   attending physician

name

mother   father

date   place

weight   height   attending physician

name

mother   father

date   place

weight   height   attending physician

name

mother   father

date   place

weight   height   attending physician

name

mother   father

date   place

weight   height   attending physician

name

mother   father

date   place

weight   height   attending physician

name

mother   father

date   place

weight   height   attending physician

name

mother   father

date   place

weight   height   attending physician

name

mother   father

date   place

weight   height   attending physician

name

mother   father

date   place

weight   height   attending physician

FAMILY DIVORCES

_____ and _____
name   name

_____
date of marriage   date of divorce

children of marriage
_____

_____ and _____
name   name

_____
date of marriage   date of divorce

children of marriage
_____

_____ and _____
name   name

_____
date of marriage   date of divorce

children of marriage
_____

_____ and _____
name   name

_____
date of marriage   date of divorce

children of marriage
_____

_____ and _____
name   name

_____
date of marriage   date of divorce

children of marriage
_____

_____ and _____
name   name

_____
date of marriage   date of divorce

children of marriage
_____

WHERE WE WORSHIPED

WHERE WE LIVED

address
_____

from _____ to _____

description of house & neighborhood
_____

address
_____

from _____ to _____

description of house & neighborhood
_____

address
_____

from _____ to _____

description of house & neighborhood
_____

address
_____

from _____ to _____

description of house & neighborhood
_____

address
_____

from _____ to _____

description of house & neighborhood
_____

address
_____

from _____ to _____

description of house & neighborhood
_____

address
_____

from _____ to _____

description of house & neighborhood
_____

address

from   to

description of house & neighborhood

address

from   to

description of house & neighborhood

address

from   to

description of house & neighborhood

address

from   to

description of house & neighborhood

address

from   to

description of house & neighborhood

address

from   to

description of house & neighborhood

address

from   to

description of house & neighborhood

address

from   to

description of house & neighborhood

address

from   to

description of house & neighborhood

address

from   to

description of house & neighborhood

address

from   to

description of house & neighborhood

address

from   to

description of house & neighborhood

address

from   to

description of house & neighborhood

address

from   to

description of house & neighborhood

address

from   to

description of house & neighborhood

address

from   to

description of house & neighborhood

address

from   to

description of house & neighborhood

address

from   to

description of house & neighborhood

address

from   to

description of house & neighborhood

address

from   to

description of house & neighborhood

address

from   to

description of house & neighborhood

WHERE WE
WENT TO SCHOOL

name

nursery school

grammar school

junior high school

high school   class of

college or university

major/minor   degree   class of

post-graduate studies

course of studies   degree   class of

name

nursery school

grammar school

junior high school

high school   class of

college or university

major/minor   degree   class of

post-graduate studies

course of studies   degree   class of

name _____

nursery school _____

grammar school _____

junior high school _____

high school _____ class of _____

college or university _____

major/minor _____ degree _____ class of _____

post-graduate studies _____

course of studies _____ degree _____ class of _____

name _____

nursery school _____

grammar school _____

junior high school _____

high school _____ class of _____

college or university _____

major/minor _____ degree _____ class of _____

post-graduate studies _____

course of studies _____ degree _____ class of _____

name _____

nursery school _____

grammar school _____

junior high school _____

high school _____ class of _____

college or university _____

major/minor _____ degree _____ class of _____

post-graduate studies _____

course of studies _____ degree _____ class of _____

name

nursery school

grammar school

junior high school

high school   class of

college or university

major/minor   degree   class of

post-graduate studies

course of studies   degree   class of

name

nursery school

grammar school

junior high school

high school   class of

college or university

major/minor   degree   class of

post-graduate studies

course of studies   degree   class of

name

nursery school

grammar school

junior high school

high school   class of

college or university

major/minor   degree   class of

post-graduate studies

course of studies   degree   class of

name

nursery school

grammar school

junior high school

high school   class of

college or university

major/minor   degree   class of

post-graduate studies

course of studies   degree   class of

name

nursery school

grammar school

junior high school

high school   class of

college or university

major/minor   degree   class of

post-graduate studies

course of studies   degree   class of

name

nursery school

grammar school

junior high school

high school   class of

college or university

major/minor   degree   class of

post-graduate studies

course of studies   degree   class of

OTHER STUDIES
& LESSONS

name

type of instruction

teacher or institution

year(s) of study

awards, accomplishments, shows, etc.

name

type of instruction

teacher or institution

year(s) of study

awards, accomplishments, shows, etc.

name

type of instruction

teacher or institution

year(s) of study

awards, accomplishments, shows, etc.

name

type of instruction

teacher or institution

year(s) of study

awards, accomplishments, shows, etc.

name

type of instruction

teacher or institution

year(s) of study

awards, accomplishments, shows, etc.

name

type of instruction

teacher or institution

year(s) of study

awards, accomplishments, shows, etc.

name

type of instruction

teacher or institution

year(s) of study

awards, accomplishments, shows, etc.

name

type of instruction

teacher or institution

year(s) of study

awards, accomplishments, shows, etc.

name

type of instruction

teacher or institution

year(s) of study

awards, accomplishments, shows, etc.

ORGANIZATIONS WE JOINED

WHERE WE WORKED

name
_____

employer _____ address _____

dates _____ to _____ from _____ job description _____

union affiliation _____ business organizations _____

name
_____

employer _____ address _____

dates _____ to _____ from _____ job description _____

union affiliation _____ business organizations _____

name
_____

employer _____ address _____

dates _____ to _____ from _____ job description _____

union affiliation _____ business organizations _____

name
_____

employer _____ address _____

dates _____ to _____ from _____ job description _____

union affiliation _____ business organizations _____

name
_____

employer _____ address _____

dates _____ to _____ from _____ job description _____

union affiliation _____ business organizations _____

name

employer   address

dates   to   from   job description

union affiliation   business organizations

name

employer   address

dates   to   from   job description

union affiliation   business organizations

name

employer   address

dates   to   from   job description

union affiliation   business organizations

name

employer   address

dates   to   from   job description

union affiliation   business organizations

name

employer   address

dates   to   from   job description

union affiliation   business organizations

name

employer   address

dates   to   from   job description

union affiliation   business organizations

name

employer   address

dates   to   from   job description

union affiliation   business organizations

name

employer   address

dates   to   from   job description

union affiliation   business organizations

name

employer   address

dates   to   from   job description

union affiliation   business organizations

name

employer   address

dates   to   from   job description

union affiliation   business organizations

name

employer   address

dates   to   from   job description

union affiliation   business organizations

name

employer   address

dates   to   from   job description

union affiliation   business organizations

name

employer   address

dates   to   from   job description

union affiliation   business organizations

name

employer   address

dates   to   from   job description

union affiliation   business organizations

name

employer   address

dates   to   from   job description

union affiliation   business organizations

name

employer   address

dates   to   from   job description

union affiliation   business organizations

name

employer   address

dates   to   from   job description

union affiliation   business organizations

name

employer   address

dates   to   from   job description

union affiliation   business organizations

SELF-EMPLOYMENT RECORD

name
_____

type of business, name & address
_____

dates _____ to _____ from _____

remarks
_____

name
_____

type of business, name & address
_____

dates _____ to _____ from _____

remarks
_____

name
_____

type of business, name & address
_____

dates _____ to _____ from _____

remarks
_____

name
_____

type of business, name & address
_____

dates _____ to _____ from _____

remarks
_____

name
_____

type of business, name & address
_____

dates _____ to _____ from _____

remarks
_____

name
_____

type of business, name & address
_____

dates   to   from
_____

remarks
_____

name
_____

type of business, name & address
_____

dates   to   from
_____

remarks
_____

name
_____

type of business, name & address
_____

dates   to   from
_____

remarks
_____

name
_____

type of business, name & address
_____

dates   to   from
_____

remarks
_____

name
_____

type of business, name & address
_____

dates   to   from
_____

remarks
_____

name
_____

type of business, name & address
_____

dates   to   from
_____

remarks
_____

PRIVATE VENTURES

name
_____

nature of venture, name & address
_____

dates   to   from
_____

remarks
_____

name
_____

nature of venture, name & address
_____

dates   to   from
_____

remarks
_____

name
_____

nature of venture, name & address
_____

dates   to   from
_____

remarks
_____

name
_____

nature of venture, name & address
_____

dates   to   from
_____

remarks
_____

name
_____

nature of venture, name & address
_____

dates   to   from
_____

remarks
_____

name

nature of venture, name & address

dates   to   from

remarks

name

nature of venture, name & address

dates   to   from

remarks

name

nature of venture, name & address

dates   to   from

remarks

name

nature of venture, name & address

dates   to   from

remarks

name

nature of venture, name & address

dates   to   from

remarks

name

nature of venture, name & address

dates   to   from

remarks

WHERE WE SERVED
OUR COUNTRY

name _____ service number _____ rank _____

inducted _____ month _____ day _____ year _____ at age _____

branch of service _____ grade _____

division _____ regiment _____ department or ship _____ dates _____

remarks _____

_____

_____

name _____ service number _____ rank _____

inducted _____ month _____ day _____ year _____ at age _____

branch of service _____ grade _____

division _____ regiment _____ department or ship _____ dates _____

remarks _____

_____

_____

name _____ service number _____ rank _____

inducted _____ month _____ day _____ year _____ at age _____

branch of service _____ grade _____

division _____ regiment _____ department or ship _____ dates _____

remarks _____

_____

_____

name   service number   rank

inducted   month   day   year   at age

branch of service   grade

division   regiment   department or ship   dates

remarks

name   service number   rank

inducted   month   day   year   at age

branch of service   grade

division   regiment   department or ship   dates

remarks

name   service number   rank

inducted   month   day   year   at age

branch of service   grade

division   regiment   department or ship   dates

remarks

name _____ service number _____ rank _____

inducted _____ month _____ day _____ year _____ at age _____

branch of service _____ grade _____

division _____ regiment _____ department or ship _____ dates _____

remarks _____

_____

_____

name _____ service number _____ rank _____

inducted _____ month _____ day _____ year _____ at age _____

branch of service _____ grade _____

division _____ regiment _____ department or ship _____ dates _____

remarks _____

_____

_____

name _____ service number _____ rank _____

inducted _____ month _____ day _____ year _____ at age _____

branch of service _____ grade _____

division _____ regiment _____ department or ship _____ dates _____

remarks _____

_____

_____

name _____ service number _____ rank _____

inducted _____ month _____ day _____ year _____ at age _____

branch of service _____ grade _____

division _____ regiment _____ department or ship _____ dates _____

remarks _____

_____

_____

name   service number   rank

inducted   month   day   year   at age

branch of service   grade

division   regiment   department or ship   dates

remarks

---

name   service number   rank

inducted   month   day   year   at age

branch of service   grade

division   regiment   department or ship   dates

remarks

---

name   service number   rank

inducted   month   day   year   at age

branch of service   grade

division   regiment   department or ship   dates

remarks

---

name   service number   rank

inducted   month   day   year   at age

branch of service   grade

division   regiment   department or ship   dates

remarks

WHERE WE CAME FROM

name

emigrated from   to   date

reasons for leaving country of origin

memories

recollections of first years here

name

emigrated from   to   date

reasons for leaving country of origin

memories

recollections of first years here

name

emigrated from   to   date

reasons for leaving country of origin

memories

recollections of first years here

name
_____

emigrated from   to   date
_____

reasons for leaving country of origin
_____
_____

memories
_____
_____

recollections of first years here
_____
_____
_____
_____

name
_____

emigrated from   to   date
_____

reasons for leaving country of origin
_____
_____

memories
_____
_____

recollections of first years here
_____
_____
_____
_____

name
_____

emigrated from   to   date
_____

reasons for leaving country of origin
_____
_____

memories
_____
_____

recollections of first years here
_____
_____
_____
_____

BEST FRIENDS

FAMILY PETS

name

breed or description

from   until

memories

name

breed or description

from   until

memories

name

breed or description

from   until

memories

name

breed or description

from   until

memories

name

breed or description

from   until

memories

name

breed or description

from   until

memories

name

breed or description

from   until

memories

name

breed or description

from   until

memories

name

breed or description

from   until

memories

name

breed or description

from   until

memories

FAMILY AUTOMOBILES

make _____ model _____

year _____ color _____

owned from _____ until _____

trips we took _____

_____

memories _____

_____

_____

make _____ model _____

year _____ color _____

owned from _____ until _____

trips we took _____

_____

memories _____

_____

_____

make _____ model _____

year _____ color _____

owned from _____ until _____

trips we took _____

_____

memories _____

_____

_____

make _____ model _____

year _____ color _____

owned from _____ until _____

trips we took _____

_____

memories _____

_____

_____

make _____ model _____

year _____ color _____

owned from _____ until _____

trips we took _____

_____

memories _____

_____

_____

make _____ model _____

year _____ color _____

owned from _____ until _____

trips we took _____

_____

memories _____

_____

_____

make   model

year   color

owned from   until

trips we took

memories

make   model

year   color

owned from   until

trips we took

memories

make   model

year   color

owned from   until

trips we took

memories

make   model

year   color

owned from   until

trips we took

memories

make   model

year   color

owned from   until

trips we took

memories

make   model

year   color

owned from   until

trips we took

memories

FAVORITE SPORTS & GAMES

FAMILY HOBBIES

FAMILY VACATIONS

SUMMER CAMP

name
_____

name of camp & location
_____

year(s) attended
_____

memories & friends
_____

name
_____

name of camp & location
_____

year(s) attended
_____

memories & friends
_____

name
_____

name of camp & location
_____

year(s) attended
_____

memories & friends
_____

name
_____

name of camp & location
_____

year(s) attended
_____

memories & friends
_____

name
_____

name of camp & location
_____

year(s) attended
_____

memories & friends
_____

name
_____

name of camp & location
_____

year(s) attended
_____

memories & friends
_____

name
_____

name of camp & location
_____

year(s) attended
_____

memories & friends
_____

name
_____

name of camp & location
_____

year(s) attended
_____

memories & friends
_____

name
_____

name of camp & location
_____

year(s) attended
_____

memories & friends
_____

name
_____

name of camp & location
_____

year(s) attended
_____

memories & friends
_____

name
_____

name of camp & location
_____

year(s) attended
_____

memories & friends
_____

name
_____

name of camp & location
_____

year(s) attended
_____

memories & friends
_____

FAMILY GATHERINGS

FAMILY TRADITIONS

HISTORIC FAMILY EVENTS

FAMILY RECORDS
& DOCUMENTS

CHECKLIST OF FAMILY RECORDS

document _____ belongs to _____

location _____

document _____ belongs to _____

location _____

document _____ belongs to _____

location _____

document _____ belongs to _____

location _____

document _____ belongs to _____

location _____

document _____ belongs to _____

location _____

document _____ belongs to _____

location _____

document _____ belongs to _____

location _____

document _____ belongs to _____

location _____

document _____ belongs to _____

location _____

document _____ belongs to _____

location _____

document _____ belongs to _____

location _____

document _____ belongs to _____

location _____

document _____ belongs to _____

location _____

document _____ belongs to _____

location _____

document _____ belongs to _____

location _____

document _____ belongs to _____

location _____

document _____ belongs to _____

location _____

document _____ belongs to _____

location _____

document _____ belongs to _____

location _____

document _____ belongs to _____

location _____

document _____ belongs to _____

location _____

document   belongs to

location

document   belongs to

location

document   belongs to

location

document   belongs to

location

document   belongs to

location

document   belongs to

location

document   belongs to

location

document   belongs to

location

document   belongs to

location

document   belongs to

location

document   belongs to

location

document _____ belongs to _____

location _____

document _____ belongs to _____

location _____

document _____ belongs to _____

location _____

document _____ belongs to _____

location _____

document _____ belongs to _____

location _____

document _____ belongs to _____

location _____

document _____ belongs to _____

location _____

document _____ belongs to _____

location _____

document _____ belongs to _____

location _____

document _____ belongs to _____

location _____

document _____ belongs to _____

location _____

document _____ belongs to _____

location _____

document   belongs to

location

document   belongs to

location

document   belongs to

location

document   belongs to

location

document   belongs to

location

document   belongs to

location

document   belongs to

location

document   belongs to

location

document   belongs to

location

document   belongs to

location

document   belongs to

location

document   belongs to

location

document   belongs to

location

document   belongs to

location

document   belongs to

location

document   belongs to

location

document   belongs to

location

document   belongs to

location

document   belongs to

location

document   belongs to

location

document   belongs to

location

document   belongs to

location

document   belongs to

location

document   belongs to

location

document _____ belongs to _____

location _____

document _____ belongs to _____

location _____

document _____ belongs to _____

location _____

document _____ belongs to _____

location _____

document _____ belongs to _____

location _____

document _____ belongs to _____

location _____

document _____ belongs to _____

location _____

document _____ belongs to _____

location _____

document _____ belongs to _____

location _____

document _____ belongs to _____

location _____

document _____ belongs to _____

location _____

document _____ belongs to _____

location _____

document _____ belongs to _____

location _____

document _____ belongs to _____

location _____

document _____ belongs to _____

location _____

document _____ belongs to _____

location _____

document _____ belongs to _____

location _____

document _____ belongs to _____

location _____

document _____ belongs to _____

location _____

document _____ belongs to _____

location _____

document _____ belongs to _____

location _____

document _____ belongs to _____

location _____

document _____ belongs to _____

location _____

document _____ belongs to _____

location _____

document _____ belongs to _____

location _____

document _____ belongs to _____

location _____

document _____ belongs to _____

location _____

document _____ belongs to _____

location _____

document _____ belongs to _____

location _____

document _____ belongs to _____

location _____

document _____ belongs to _____

location _____

document _____ belongs to _____

location _____

document _____ belongs to _____

location _____

document _____ belongs to _____

location _____

document _____ belongs to _____

location _____

document   belongs to

location

document   belongs to

location

document   belongs to

location

document   belongs to

location

document   belongs to

location

document   belongs to

location

document   belongs to

location

document   belongs to

location

document   belongs to

location

document   belongs to

location

document   belongs to

location

HEIRLOOMS & FAMILY POSSESSIONS

description   belongs to

location

description   belongs to

location

description   belongs to

location

description   belongs to

location

description   belongs to

location

description   belongs to

location

description   belongs to

location

description   belongs to

location

description   belongs to

location

description   belongs to

location

description   belongs to

location

description   belongs to

location

description   belongs to

location

description   belongs to

location

description   belongs to

location

description   belongs to

location

description   belongs to

location

description   belongs to

location

description   belongs to

location

description   belongs to

location

description   belongs to

location

description   belongs to

location

description   belongs to

location

description   belongs to

location

description   belongs to

location

description   belongs to

location

description   belongs to

location

description   belongs to

location

description   belongs to

location

description   belongs to

location

description   belongs to

location

description   belongs to

location

description   belongs to

location

description   belongs to

location

description   belongs to

location

description   belongs to

location

description   belongs to

location

description   belongs to

location

description   belongs to

location

description   belongs to

location

description   belongs to

location

description   belongs to

location

description   belongs to

location

description   belongs to

location

description   belongs to

location

description   belongs to

location

description   belongs to

location

description   belongs to

location

description   belongs to

location

description   belongs to

location

description   belongs to

location

description   belongs to

location

description   belongs to

location

description   belongs to

location

description   belongs to

location

description   belongs to

location

description   belongs to

location

description   belongs to

location

description   belongs to

location

description   belongs to

location

description   belongs to

location

description   belongs to

location

description   belongs to

location

description   belongs to

location

description   belongs to

location

description   belongs to

location

description   belongs to

location

description   belongs to

location

description   belongs to

location

INVESTMENTS & MAJOR PURCHASES

description _____ belongs to _____

value/cost _____ maturity _____

location _____

description _____ belongs to _____

value/cost _____ maturity _____

location _____

description _____ belongs to _____

value/cost _____ maturity _____

location _____

description _____ belongs to _____

value/cost _____ maturity _____

location _____

description _____ belongs to _____

value/cost _____ maturity _____

location _____

description _____ belongs to _____

value/cost _____ maturity _____

location _____

description   belongs to

value/cost   maturity

location

description   belongs to

value/cost   maturity

location

description   belongs to

value/cost   maturity

location

description   belongs to

value/cost   maturity

location

description   belongs to

value/cost   maturity

location

description   belongs to

value/cost   maturity

location

description   belongs to

value/cost   maturity

location

MEMORABILIA

description   belongs to

location

description   belongs to

location

description   belongs to

location

description   belongs to

location

description   belongs to

location

description   belongs to

location

description   belongs to

location

description   belongs to

location

description   belongs to

location

description   belongs to

location

description   belongs to

location

description   belongs to

location

description   belongs to

location

description   belongs to

location

description   belongs to

location

description   belongs to

location

description   belongs to

location

description   belongs to

location

description   belongs to

location

description   belongs to

location

description   belongs to

location

description   belongs to

location

description   belongs to

location

description   belongs to

location

description   belongs to

location

description   belongs to

location

description   belongs to

location

description   belongs to

location

description   belongs to

location

description   belongs to

location

description   belongs to

location

description   belongs to

location

description   belongs to

location

description   belongs to

location

description   belongs to

location

description   belongs to

location

description   belongs to

location

description   belongs to

location

description   belongs to

location

description   belongs to

location

description   belongs to

location

description   belongs to

location

description   belongs to

location

description   belongs to

location

description   belongs to

location

description   belongs to

location

description   belongs to

location

FAMILY VALUABLES

description   belongs to
_____   _____
location
_____

description   belongs to
_____   _____
location
_____

description   belongs to
_____   _____
location
_____

description   belongs to
_____   _____
location
_____

description   belongs to
_____   _____
location
_____

description   belongs to
_____   _____
location
_____

description   belongs to
_____   _____
location
_____

description   belongs to
_____   _____
location
_____

description   belongs to
_____   _____
location
_____

description   belongs to
_____   _____
location
_____

description   belongs to
_____   _____
location
_____

description   belongs to

location

description   belongs to

location

description   belongs to

location

description   belongs to

location

description   belongs to

location

description   belongs to

location

description   belongs to

location

description   belongs to

location

description   belongs to

location

description   belongs to

location

description   belongs to

location

description   belongs to

location

FAMILY
MEDICAL HISTORY

name _____ date of birth _____

height _____ weight _____ eyes _____

hair _____ general description _____

serious illnesses or operations _____

date and cause of death _____

name _____ date of birth _____

height _____ weight _____ eyes _____

hair _____ general description _____

serious illnesses or operations _____

date and cause of death _____

name _____ date of birth _____

height _____ weight _____ eyes _____

hair _____ general description _____

serious illnesses or operations _____

date and cause of death _____

name _____ date of birth _____

height _____ weight _____ eyes _____

hair _____ general description _____
_____

serious illnesses or operations _____
_____

date and cause of death _____

name _____ date of birth _____

height _____ weight _____ eyes _____

hair _____ general description _____
_____

serious illnesses or operations _____
_____

date and cause of death _____

name _____ date of birth _____

height _____ weight _____ eyes _____

hair _____ general description _____
_____

serious illnesses or operations _____
_____

date and cause of death _____

name _____ date of birth _____

height _____ weight _____ eyes _____

hair _____ general description _____
_____

serious illnesses or operations _____
_____

date and cause of death _____

name _____ date of birth _____

height _____ weight _____ eyes _____

hair _____ general description _____

_____

serious illnesses or operations _____

_____

date and cause of death _____

_____

name _____ date of birth _____

height _____ weight _____ eyes _____

hair _____ general description _____

_____

serious illnesses or operations _____

_____

date and cause of death _____

_____

name _____ date of birth _____

height _____ weight _____ eyes _____

hair _____ general description _____

_____

serious illnesses or operations _____

_____

date and cause of death _____

_____

name _____ date of birth _____

height _____ weight _____ eyes _____

hair _____ general description _____

_____

serious illnesses or operations _____

_____

date and cause of death _____

_____

name   date of birth

height   weight   eyes

hair   general description

serious illnesses or operations

date and cause of death

name   date of birth

height   weight   eyes

hair   general description

serious illnesses or operations

date and cause of death

name   date of birth

height   weight   eyes

hair   general description

serious illnesses or operations

date and cause of death

name   date of birth

height   weight   eyes

hair   general description

serious illnesses or operations

date and cause of death

CEMETERY RECORDS

name _____

date of death _____

burial place _____

_____

name _____

date of death _____

burial place _____

_____

name _____

date of death _____

burial place _____

_____

name _____

date of death _____

burial place _____

_____

name _____

date of death _____

burial place _____

_____

name _____

date of death _____

burial place _____

_____

name

date of death

burial place

name

date of death

burial place

name

date of death

burial place

name

date of death

burial place

name

date of death

burial place

name

date of death

burial place

name

date of death

burial place

FAMILY INTERVIEWS

FAMILY AUTHORITIES

name & address

authority on subjects/people

remarks

name & address

authority on subjects/people

remarks

name & address

authority on subjects/people

remarks

name & address

authority on subjects/people

remarks

name & address

authority on subjects/people

remarks

name & address

authority on subjects/people

remarks

name & address

authority on subjects/people

remarks

name & address

authority on subjects/people

remarks

name & address

authority on subjects/people

remarks

name & address

authority on subjects/people

remarks

name & address

authority on subjects/people

remarks

name & address

authority on subjects/people

remarks

name & address

authority on subjects/people

remarks

name & address

authority on subjects/people

remarks

ORAL HISTORY

ORAL HISTORY

ORAL HISTORY

AUTOGRAPHS

PHOTOGRAPHS

PHOTOGRAPHS

PHOTOGRAPHS